1 4 1
2 3 2.
3 2 3
(4) 2 4
(5) 1 1 1 X 4 3 2 .
(6) 2 2 2
(7) 3 3 3.
(8) 4 4 4 X # 2 3 4 4 1
1 3 5
2 4 2
3 3 3
4 5 4
5 3 1
(6) 1 5 3
(7) 2 2 2
(8) 3 5 1
AF386592

BRIDGET RILEY

CIRCLES COLOUR STRUCTURE

STUDIES 1970/71

BRIDGET RILEY

CIRCLES COLOUR STRUCTURE

STUDIES 1970/71

Ridinghouse / Karsten Schubert
London 2008

In Conversation with Robert Kudielka [1972]

You are one of the few artists today who make preparatory studies. Why don't you work on the canvas directly?

Well, that would be impossible for me because the structure of my paintings has to be precisely balanced. They need immaculate execution. I have to build up a bank of visual information first – about colours, forms, proportions, directions, etc. This is the essential basis to my work.

What returns are there from this 'bank'?

The studies I make have different purposes. At the beginning I try to be as unselective as possible – to allow things to happen, later gradually tightening up until all aspects have been drawn together.

How do you find your direction in this process?

I proceed by trial and error – exploring and slowly establishing a particular situation. Obviously many studies will be discarded en route to a painting, though they may still be interesting as visual statements.

And yet, there is a difference between a study and a painting . . .

There are several differences. The studies deal with aspects, the painting with totality. The studies are flexible and malleable, whereas the paintings are decisive and finite. And, of course, there is the obvious difference of scale.

What does scale mean to you?

Maybe scale could be compared to a key in music. Scale is not simply size, although size is a factor of scale. Changing the size of an image always means recreating its scale. I have to readjust and rebalance the factors involved. It is an act of perceptual equation. Sitting at your table and working on a study is quite different from your response to a painting which is hanging on the wall. There is no possibility of enlarging it automatically.

If scale is the key in which your work is notated, what theme are you playing? Is it in the air or do you invent it?

No – I take *something* – a colour – say yellow. What is yellow? Merely a name, an inert notion. But if you put a yellow with other colours, in different proportions and positions, it starts to show a certain potential. It may appear lighter or darker, expand or flow into other colours, changing them. It could glow, advance or recede and so on. None of this behaviour you would know until you try. So right at the beginning I think . . . well, I just see what yellow can do.

What about the forms you use?

When I started, around 1960, forms such as triangles, squares, circles, rhomboids, etc., were no longer burdened by the heavy load of associations and symbolic overtones which they had carried in the Twenties and Thirties as Constructivist motifs. They were simple forms without any pretentions, in a condition for working with. Just 'to hand'.

Yet there has been a change. The more you got involved with colour, the less distinctive the forms became.

In my recent colour work I have been using stripes, either parallel or twisting around each other, because they are unassertive forms. Form and colour seem to be fundamentally incompatible – they destroy each other. In my earlier work, when I was developing complex forms, the energies of the medium could only be fully released by simplifying colour to a black-and-white constant (with occasional grey sequences). Conversely colour energies need a virtually neutral vehicle if they are to develop uninhibitedly. The repeated stripe seems to meet these conditions.

You think that a more elaborate shape would not be suitable?

No. Take a green triangle – it has three points, three conflicting directions, there is a central volume in the form and an active edge exposure: all these factors add up to complexities which would effectively inhibit the green's expansion and mutability. I have always tried to avoid 'colouring forms'. I want to create a colour-form, not coloured forms.

Are you concerned with perceptual principles?

Well, look at the paintings. I'm not demonstrating any scientific principle, nor perceptual, arithmetical or geometrical. That doesn't interest me at all.

I wonder what the context is within which you work?

Relationships such as constancy and change – contrast and harmony – identity and contradiction – directions – rhythm – pace – repetition accumulating and dispersing density.

Let's take an example. What does the oval mean to you?

In a sense the oval is a directional circle. Its range lies between the emphasis on direction on one hand (at the expense of its circularity), and emphasis on circularity (at the expense of direction) on the other. An oval is very different in character at each extreme. When it is highly directional it is a light, fast form. As the directional aspect decreases the oval becomes heavy and static.

But surely these dynamic relationships are not confined to single forms?

Of course not. It is very important that each form finally relinquishes its separateness in the whole. It must be fully absorbed. So while it is necessary in the early stages to analyse each unit, my aim is to enable it to release sufficient energy to precipitate its dissolution in totality.

So the single forms are the means to create a total situation?

They are part of the medium with which I am working.

Well, what is the medium?

Superficially the medium seems to be identical with

the means. And obviously this is true in a sense that, for the composer, actual notes or particular instruments are part of his medium. But the medium as a whole is the relationship of this sort of means between themselves and me. I am, like the musician, a kind of 'listener-in'– overhearing potential activities.

'Listener'– that's a beautiful description, and a paradox, too. Because in this case the listener is also the speaker. After all, you make the paintings.

Yes – for quite a long time I was embarrassed by using the word 'I', the first person, in relation to my work – I much preferred to say 'one', because I felt that this thing, the medium, was so strong and rich, that I was just an agent who caught these various inflections and allowed them to play their own thing – freely.

What do you mean, to allow things to 'play freely'?

When these elements are *not* asked to do something which is against their nature – (not asked to serve concepts or to represent) – *then* I think that they are allowed to 'play freely' – to show their vitality. But there are hazards, for instance, of merely recording automatically in a random kind of way. These energies are, in a proper sense, 'wild' – one can easily be overwhelmed, carried away. This results in images which are virtually inaccessible, beyond perception, in fact. And yet this is the *core* of the medium and it is in this area that fruitful dialogue takes place. It is not only a one-way relationship of taming the wild, but can also be the reverse. I am supported by the medium but at the risk of being overwhelmed by it – the medium both carries you and threatens to carry

you away. I don't trust a painting unless it has had this period – it is the only route by which to avoid the decorative or the academic.

The opposite of the wild would be the decorative?

Yes, the known, which is easy to handle, easy to arrange, because you are completely familiar with the relationships. Their vitality has been sapped their energy used up – their teeth, so to speak, have been drawn.

I wonder how far this polarity of the medium affects the spectator. The subject of your earlier black and white work for instance, is movement . . .

There are at least two forms of movement. The 'one-dimensional' movement, which has to do with progression. Movement described on the picture plane itself.

It's readable –

Yes – but as you look at the painting you become involved in another kind of movement as a total experience which happens in time, successively, between you and the canvas – the graphic movement anticipates this kind of experience.

So in one case it is traditional, descriptive movement, like Futurism, movement opposed to stability. The other is movement not opposed to stability but occurring simultaneously – in a sense, even provoked by stability, as in *Descending*.

That's perfectly true. And this interplay between

movement and stability is paralleled in my recent work by the interplay of light and colour. The colours painted on the canvas can be identified as certain hues – but as one looks at the painting one sees a luminous disembodied light, variously coloured.[1]

I see, you don't 'describe' light by colour.

No, I don't paint light. I present a colour situation which releases light as you look at it.

That means that the painting doesn't exist *factually*.

No, in a way, it only comes to life when looked at from a certain distance.

If you stand close to the canvas you just see the colour –

Yes objective hues, say cerise, olive, turquoise –

But if you stand too far away from the painting?

You only see a nebulous grey. The painting has eluded you.

And between these two extremes – the experience you intend?

The area of activity – of light.

So light is also something which happens between two polarities: the stable body of colour –

And its absolute dissolution. When grey eclipses the light, the painting is unable to offer anything.[2]

Is that how the spectator experiences the medium?

Well, he is probably caught in an dialogue similar to my own. It is interesting to watch people looking at a painting because without any prompting they try to relate to it – they try to find a position in which the thing works for them. A point from which they can experience it. People vary a little – as to how much or how little they can be involved they unconsciously choose their own relationship to the painting.

Do they choose? They listen.

Yes – to let the painting speak.

NOTES

1 The following references to the 'disembodied light' brought about by periodic colour structures are related to paintings like *Late Morning* (1967) and *Orient 4* (1970).

2 This early reference to the critical role of distance in colour perception has been extended in Riley's radio conversation with E.H. Gombrich, see *Dialogues on Art*, p. 44.

Position Study: Red and Blue Open Discs 1970
Gouache and pencil on paper
27¼ × 40 inches

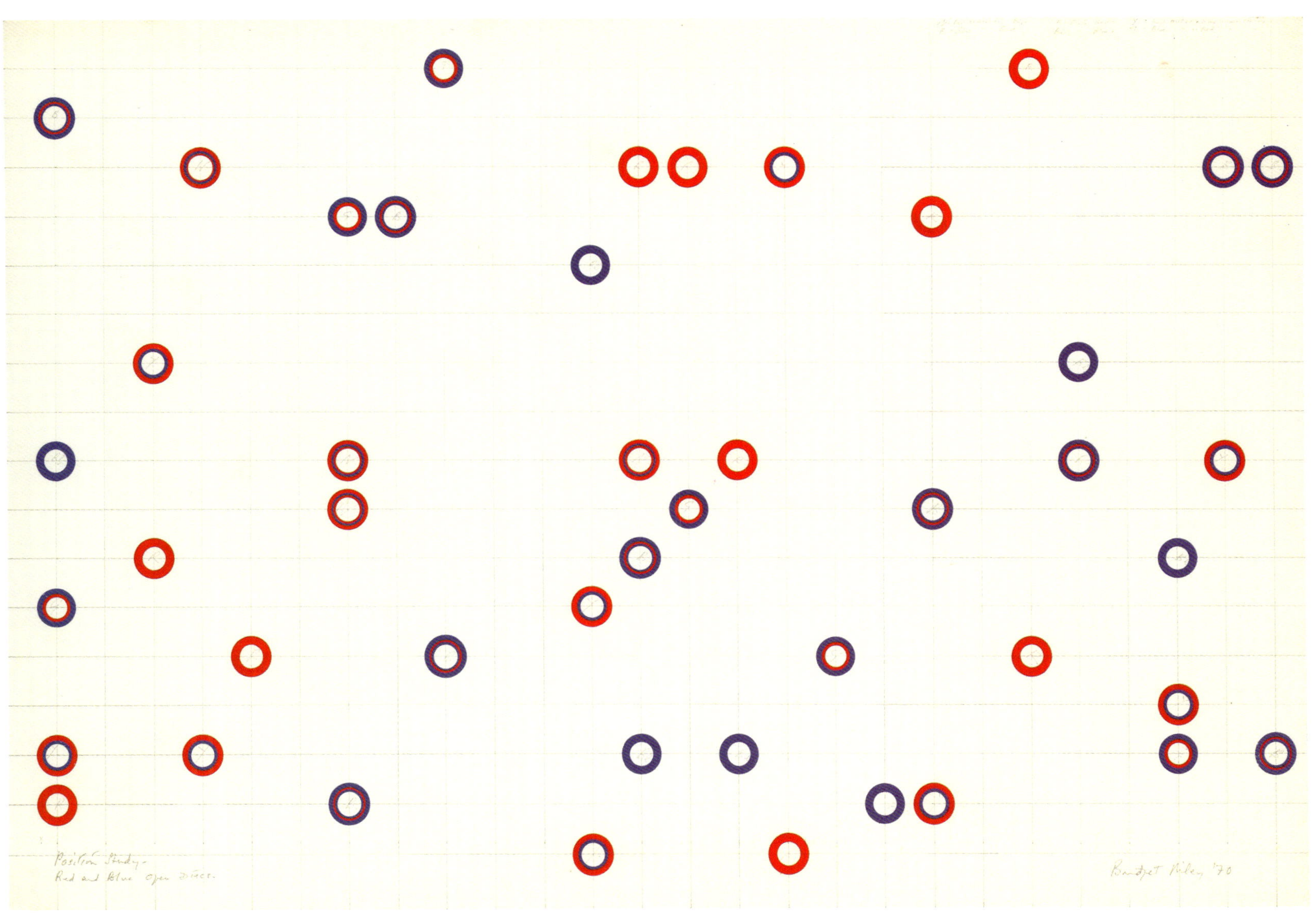

Position Study.
Red and Blue Open Discs.
Bridget Riley '70

Red and Blue Open Discs 1970
Gouache and pencil on paper
24½ × 37¼ inches

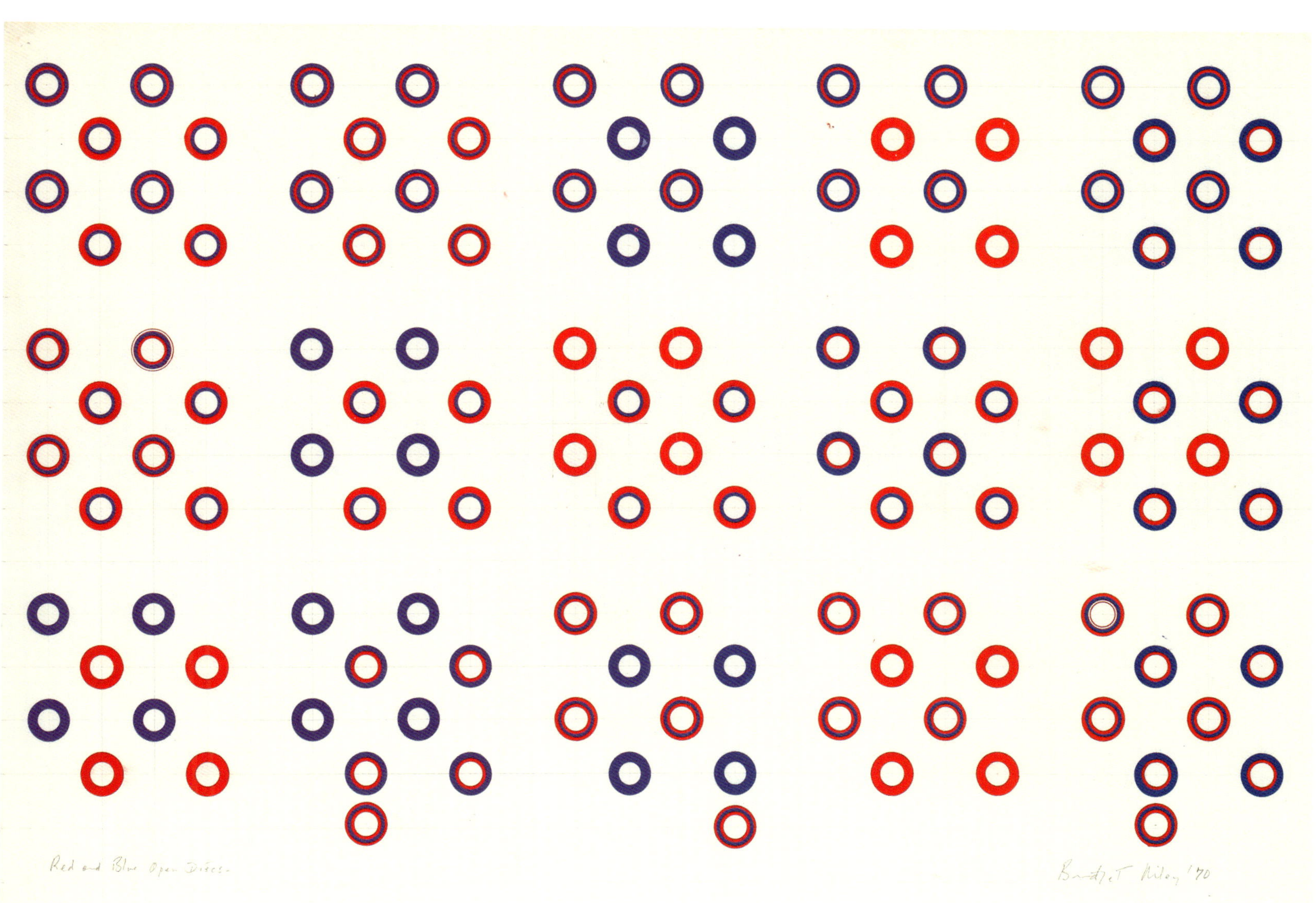

Red and Blue Open Discs
Bridget Riley '70

Red and Blue Open Discs 1970
Gouache on paper
12½ × 25 inches

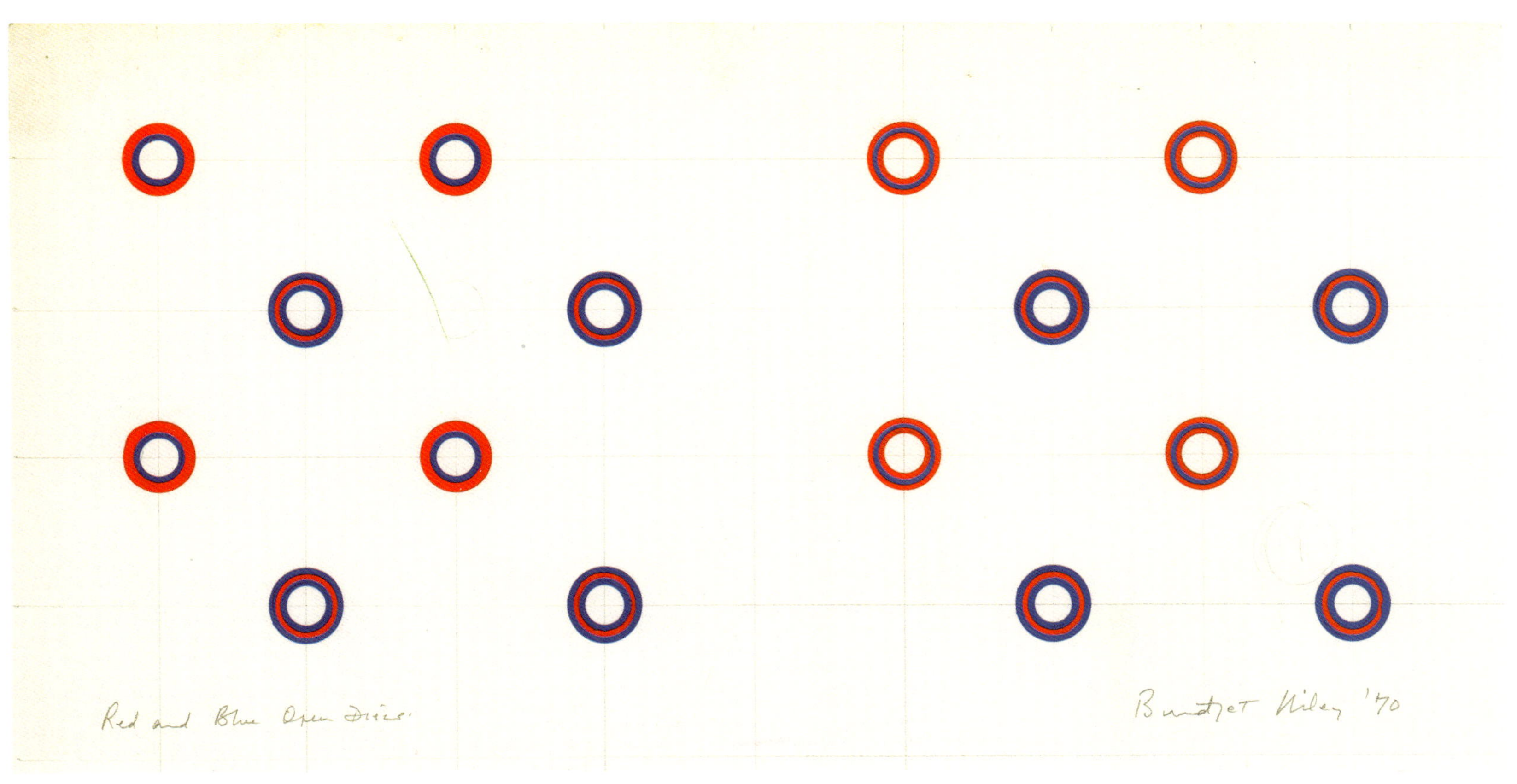

Red and Blue Open Discs.
Bridget Riley '70

Untitled 1970
Gouache and pencil on paper
13½ × 12 inches

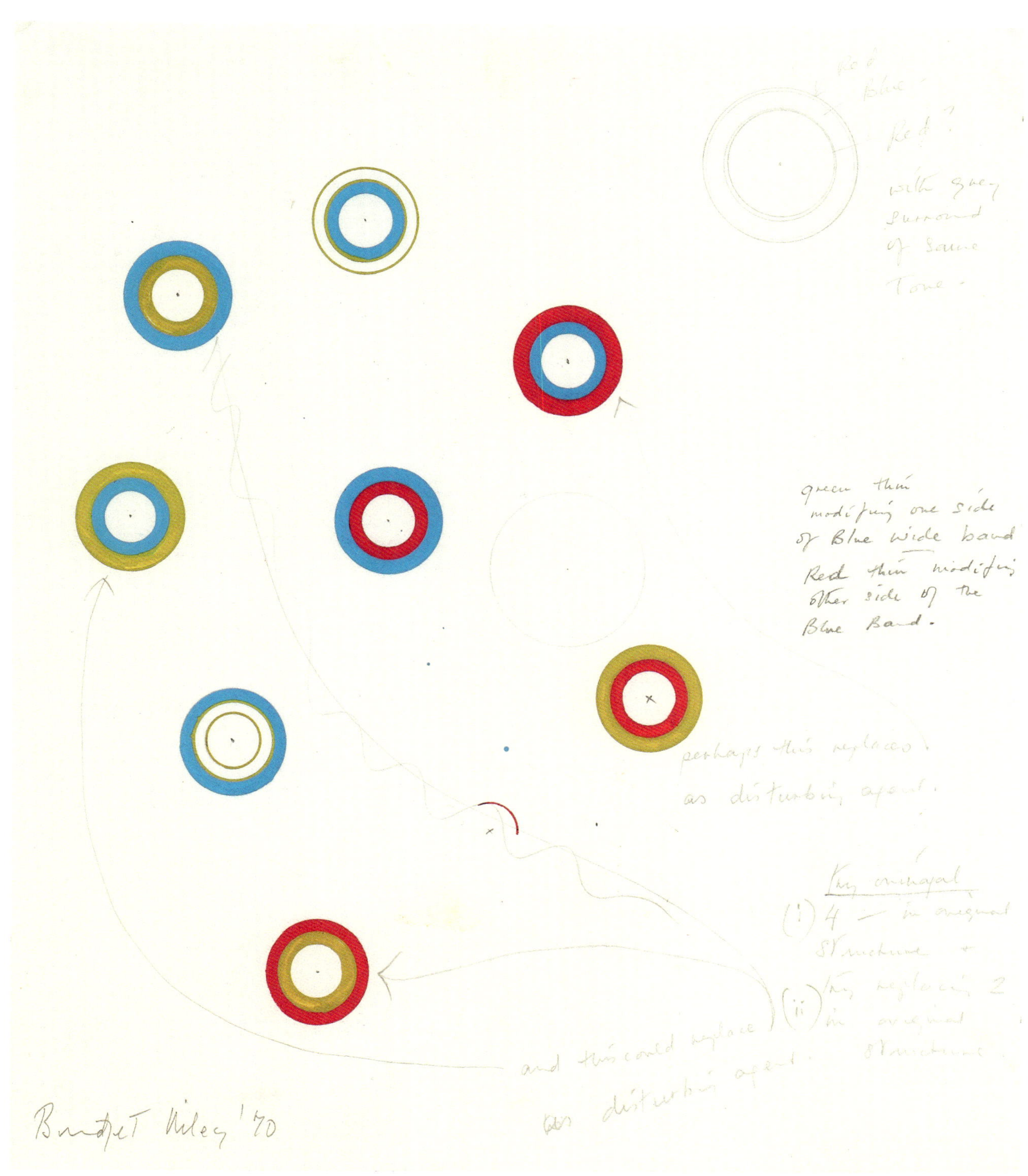

green thin
modifying one side
of Blue wide band
Red thin modifying
other side of the
Blue Band.

perhaps this replaced
as disturbing agent.

This original
(i) 4 — in original
structure +
(ii) this replacing 2
in original
structure.

and this could replace
as disturbing agent.

Bridget Riley '70

Turquoise, Cerise, Ochre: Closed Discs with Black 1970
Gouache and pencil on graph paper
25¾ × 23 inches

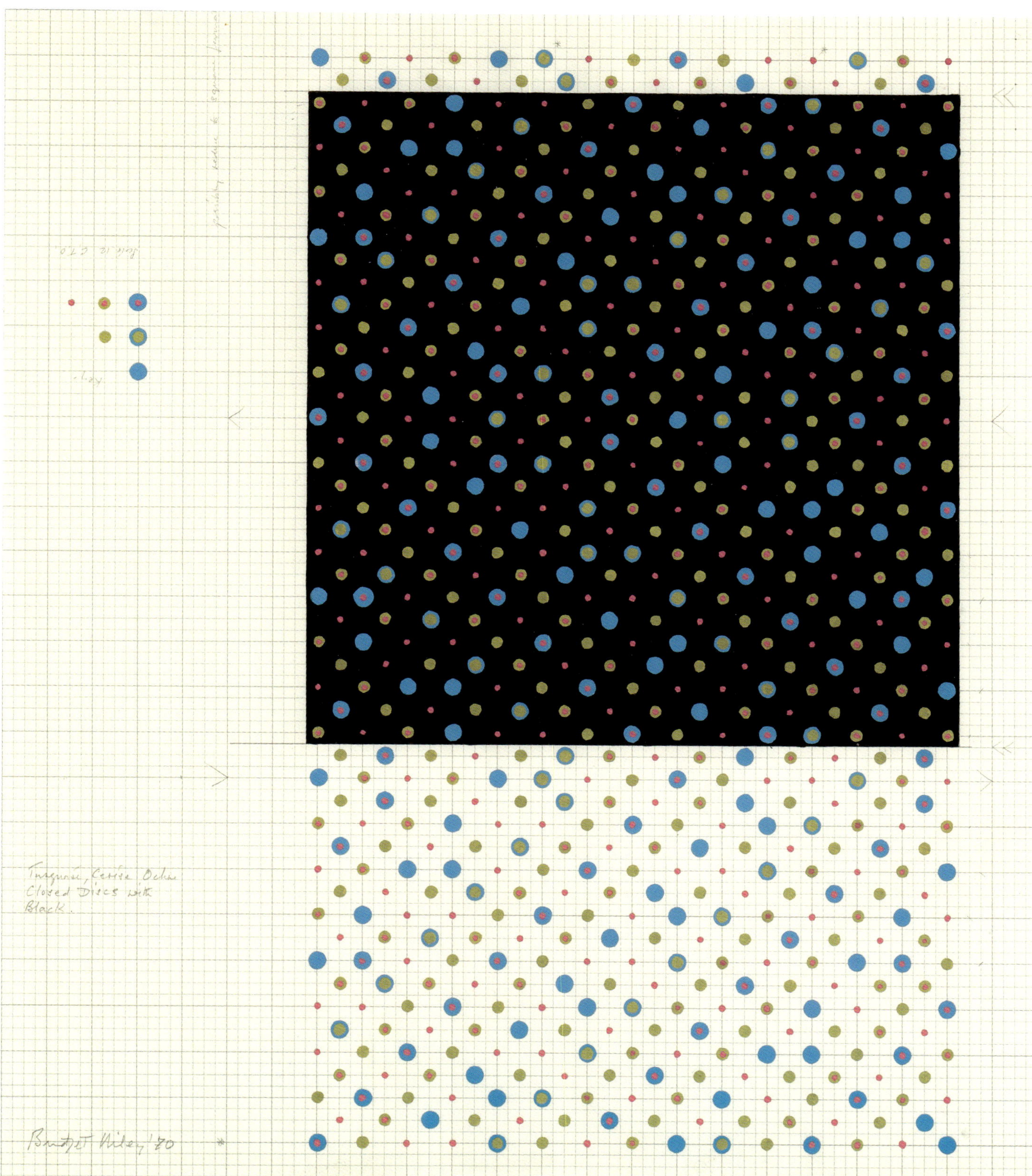

Scale Study: Ochre, Cerise and Turquoise in Closed Discs 1970
Gouache and pencil on graph paper
28 × 41 inches

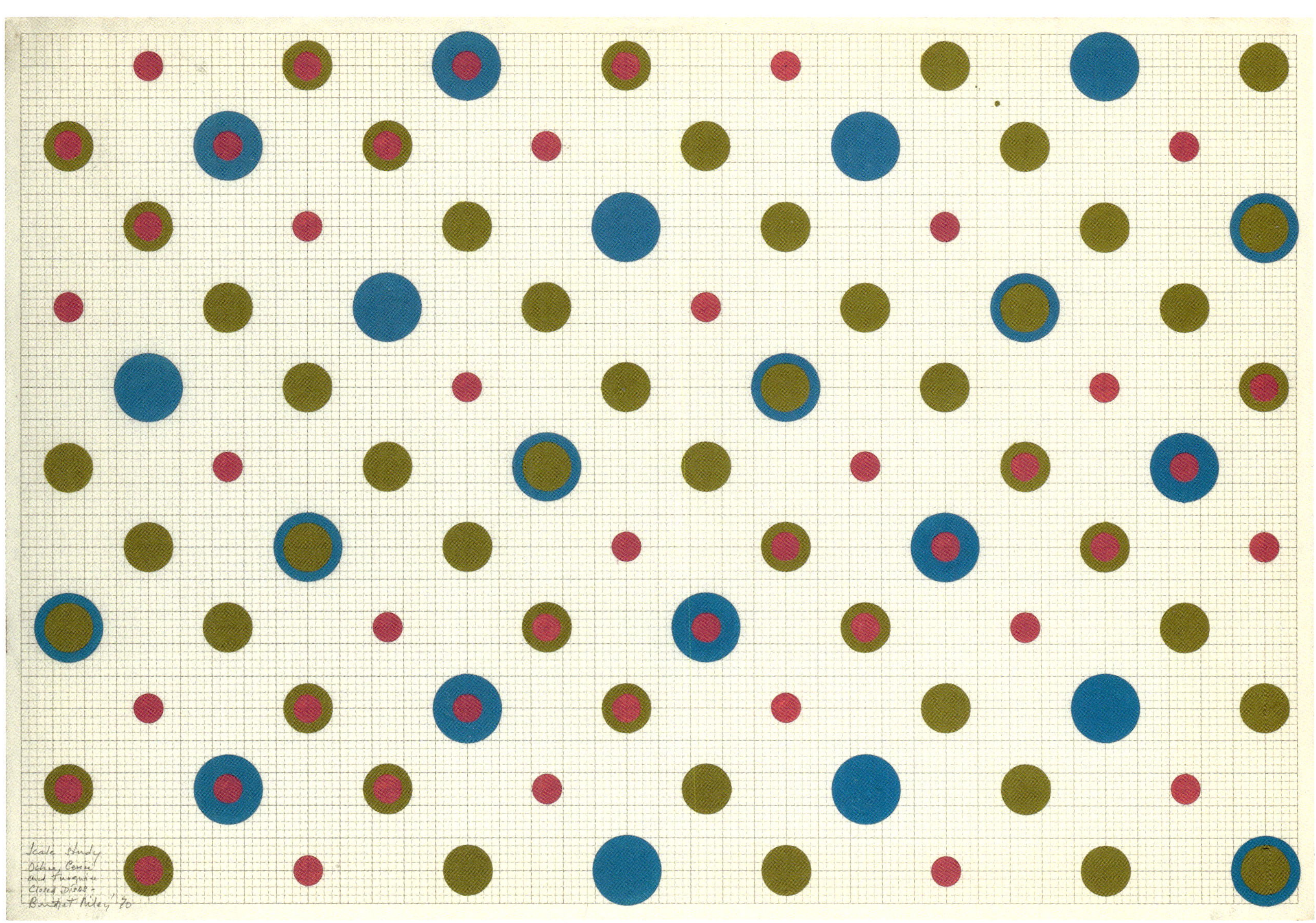
Scale Study
Ochre, Cerise
and Turquoise
Coloured Discs:
Bridget Riley '70

Untitled 1970
Gouache on graph paper
11¾ × 20 inches

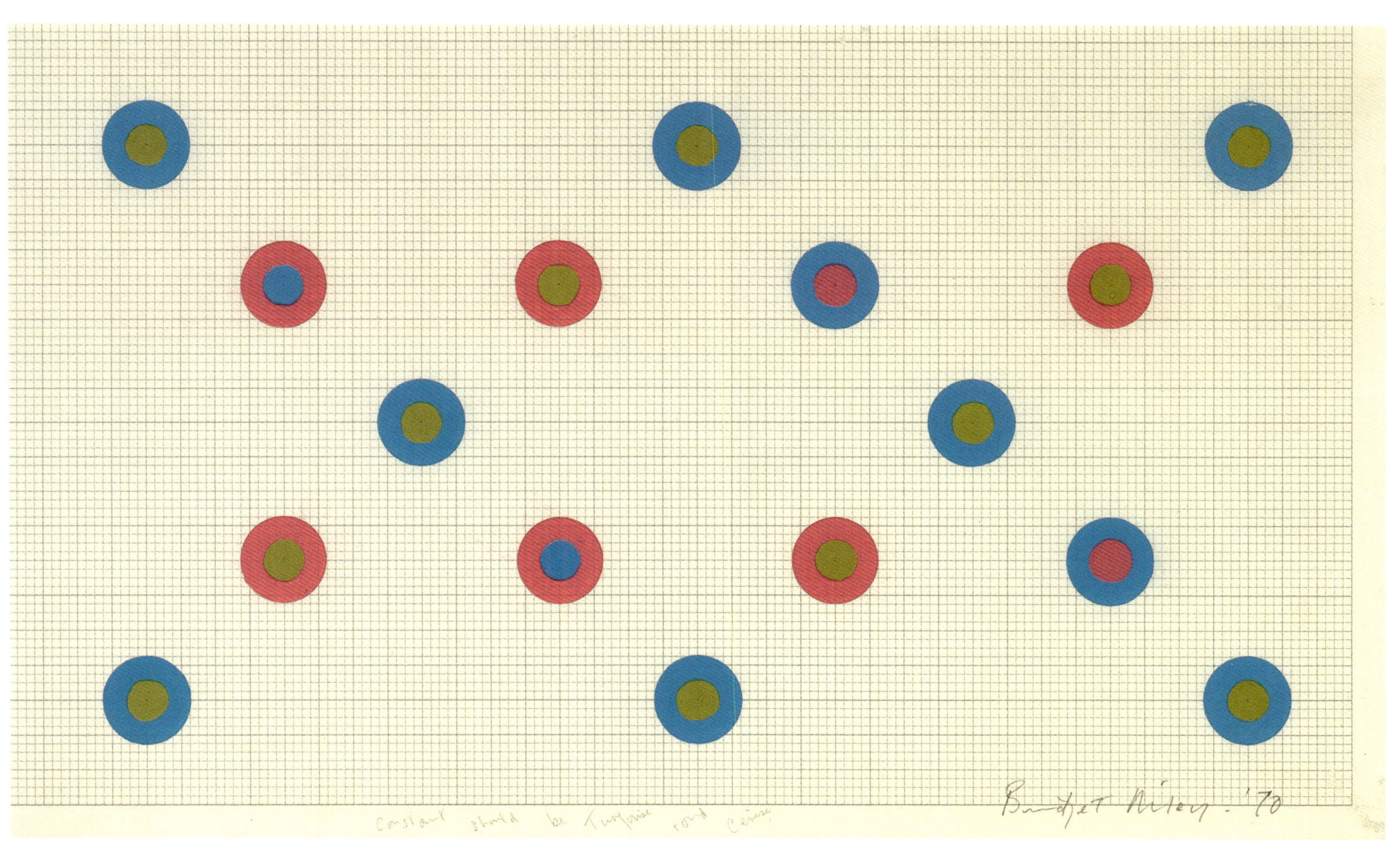

Constant should be Turquoise rond Cerise.
Bridget Riley. '70

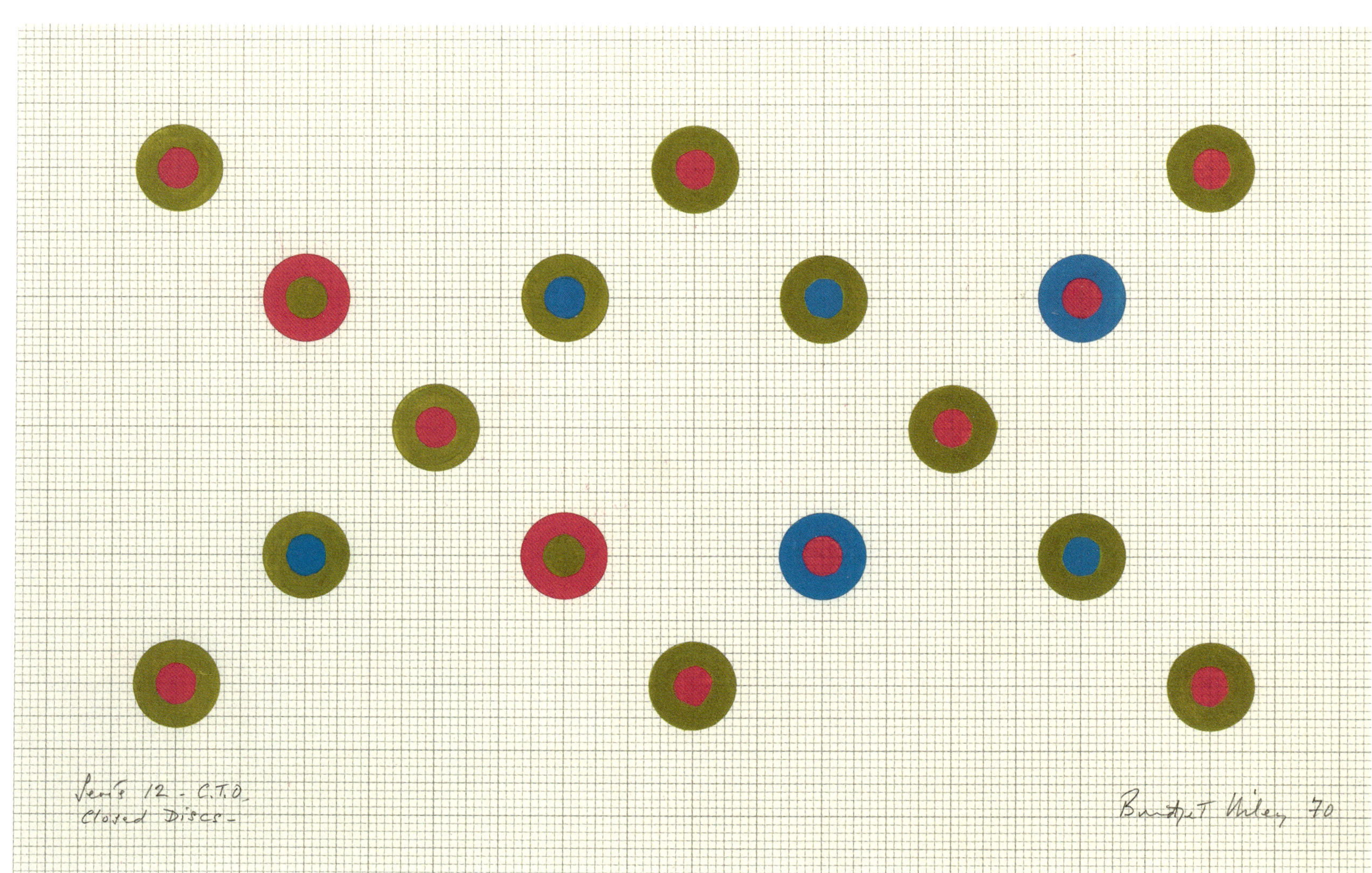

Series 12: C T O, Closed Discs 1970
Gouache on graph paper
13¼ × 21 inches

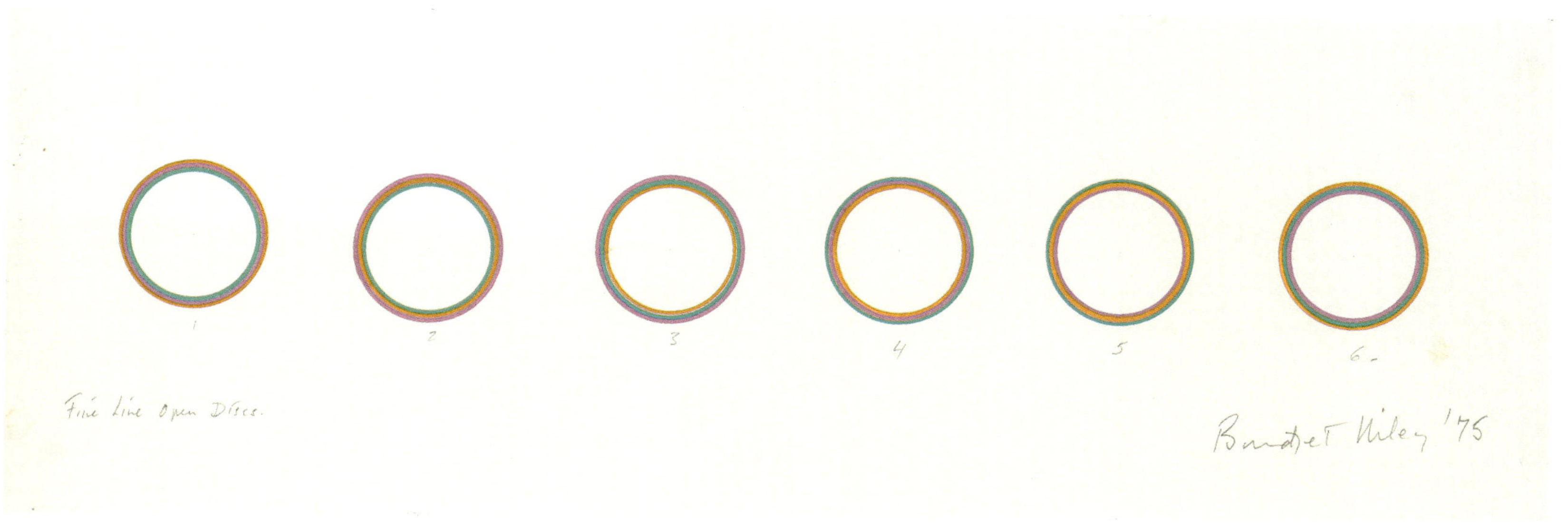

Fine Line Open Discs 1975
Gouache and pencil on paper
8¾ × 27¼ inches

**Series 1: Pacing Juxtapositions, Red Constant
Plus Blue to Green Sequence** 1970
Gouache and pencil on graph paper
20½ × 28 inches

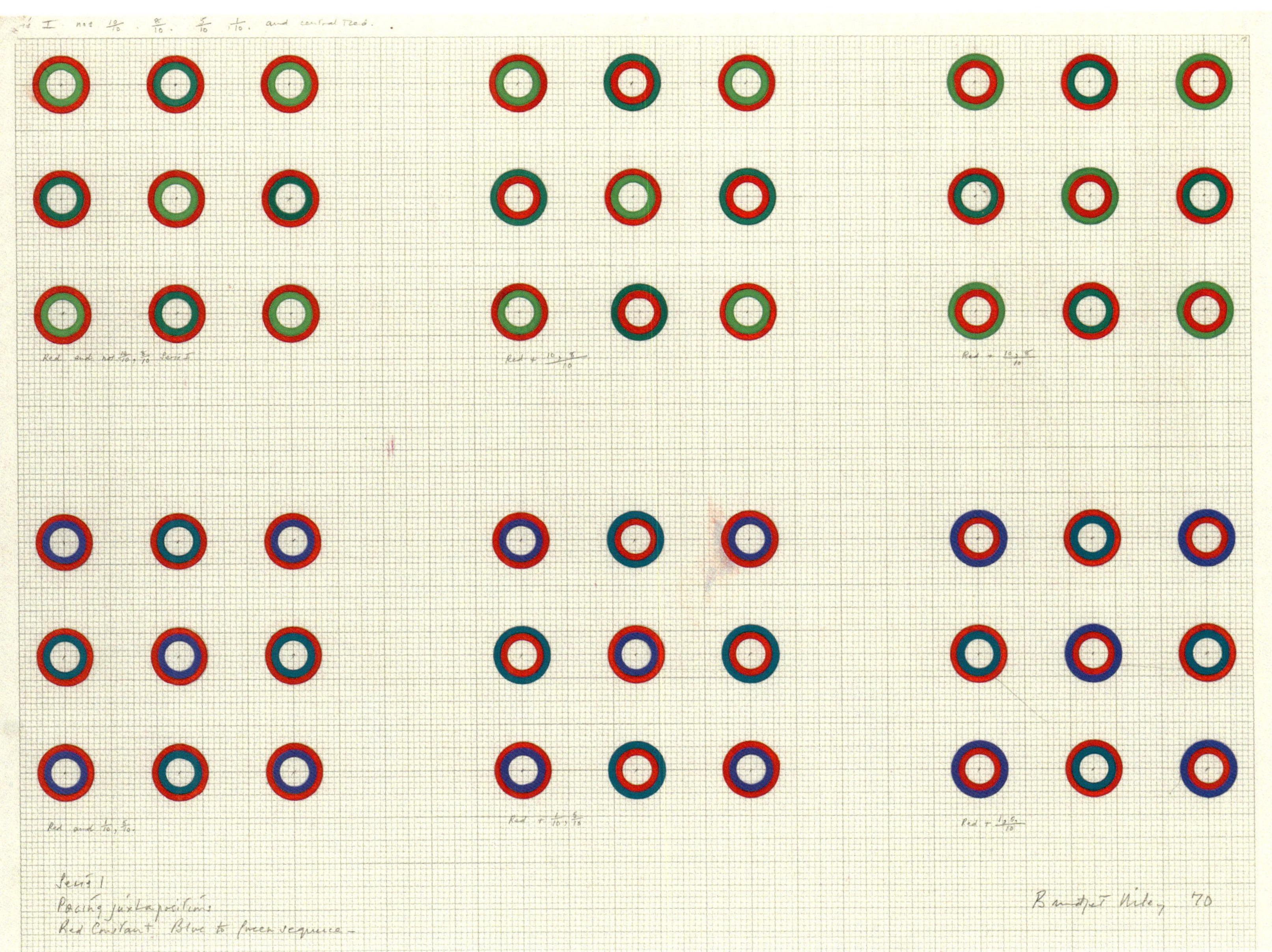
nos 10/10. 8/10. 5/10. 1/10. and central red.
Series 1
Pacing juxtapositions
Red Constant Blue to Green sequence —
Bridget Riley 70

Series 1: Red Constant, Blue to Green Sequence 1970
Gouache on graph paper
7½ × 25½ inches

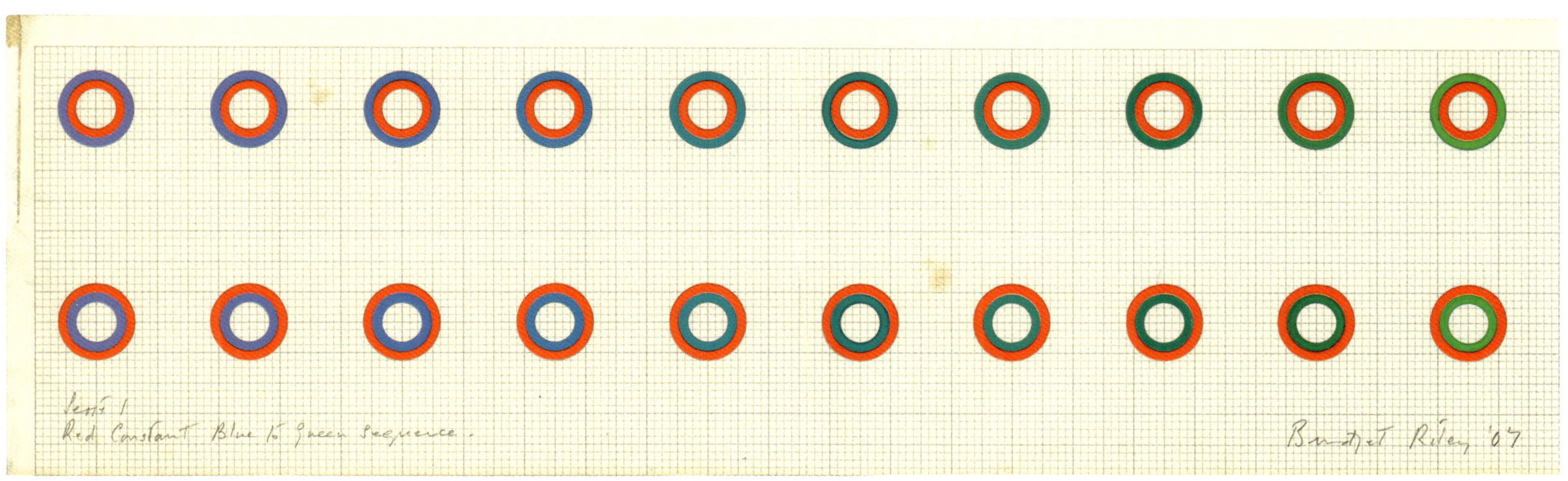

Test 1
Red Constant Blue to Green Sequence.
Bridget Riley '67

Oval Axis: Cerise, Turquoise, Ochre 1970
Gouache and pencil on paper
12 × 26 inches

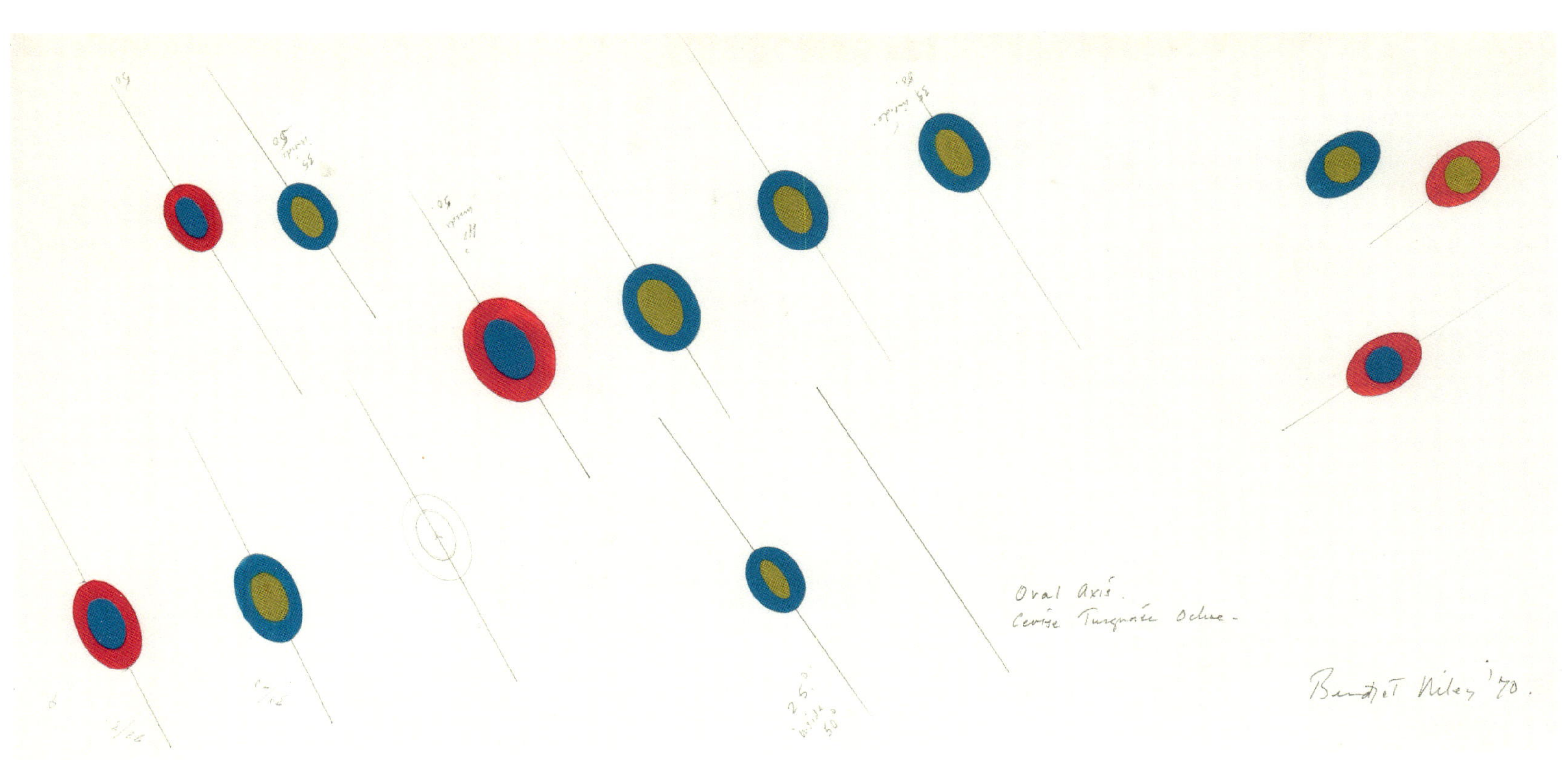

Oval axis.
Cerise Turquoise Ochre.
Bridget Riley '70.

Untitled 1970
Gouache on paper
12 × 23⅜ inches

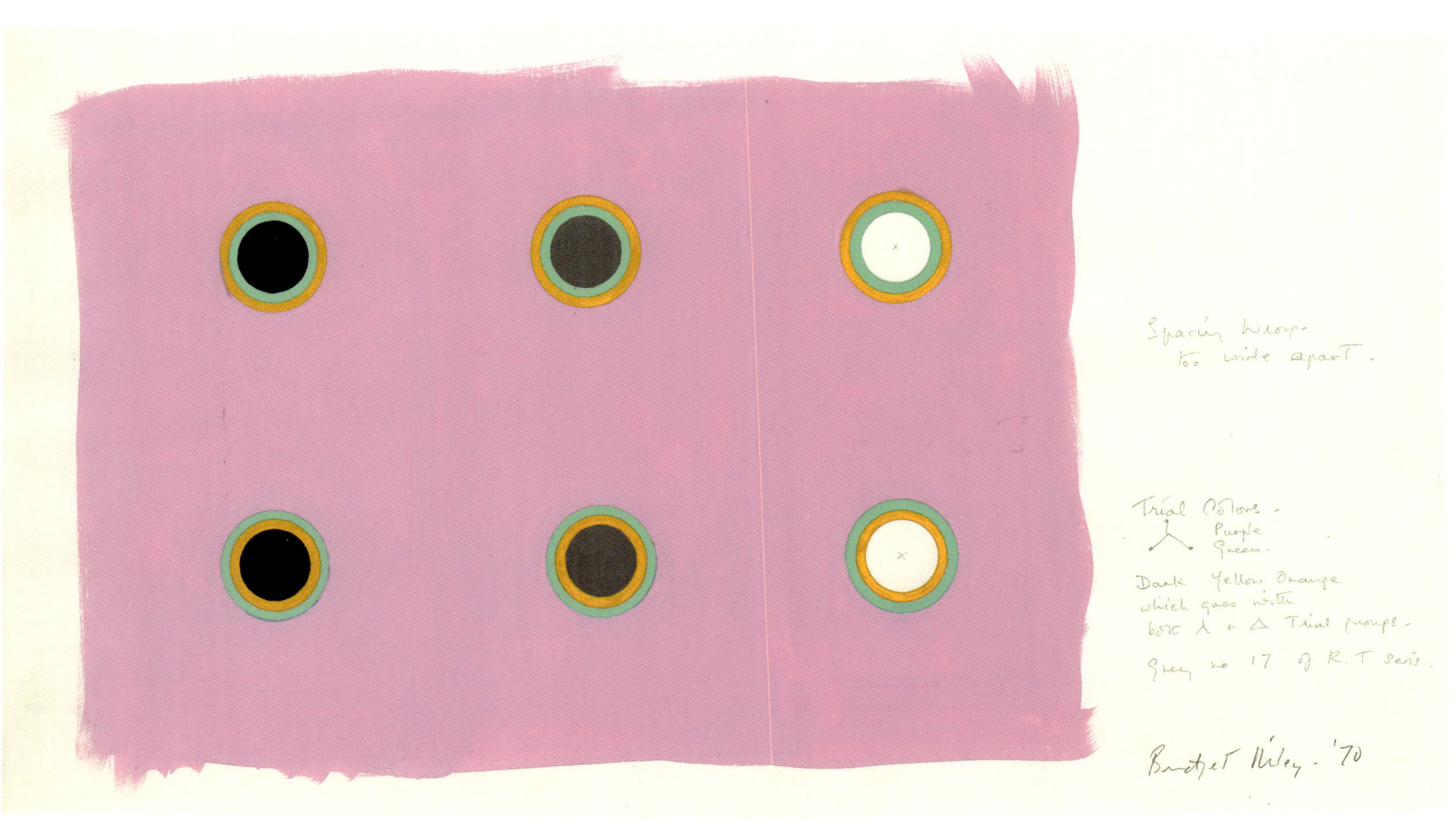

Spacing Wrong -
too wide apart.

Trial Colours -
Purple
Green -
Dark Yellow Orange
which goes with
both λ + △ Trial groups -
grey no 17 of R.T series.

Bridget Riley - '70

Encircling Discs 1971
Gouache and pencil on graph paper
15 × 27½ inches

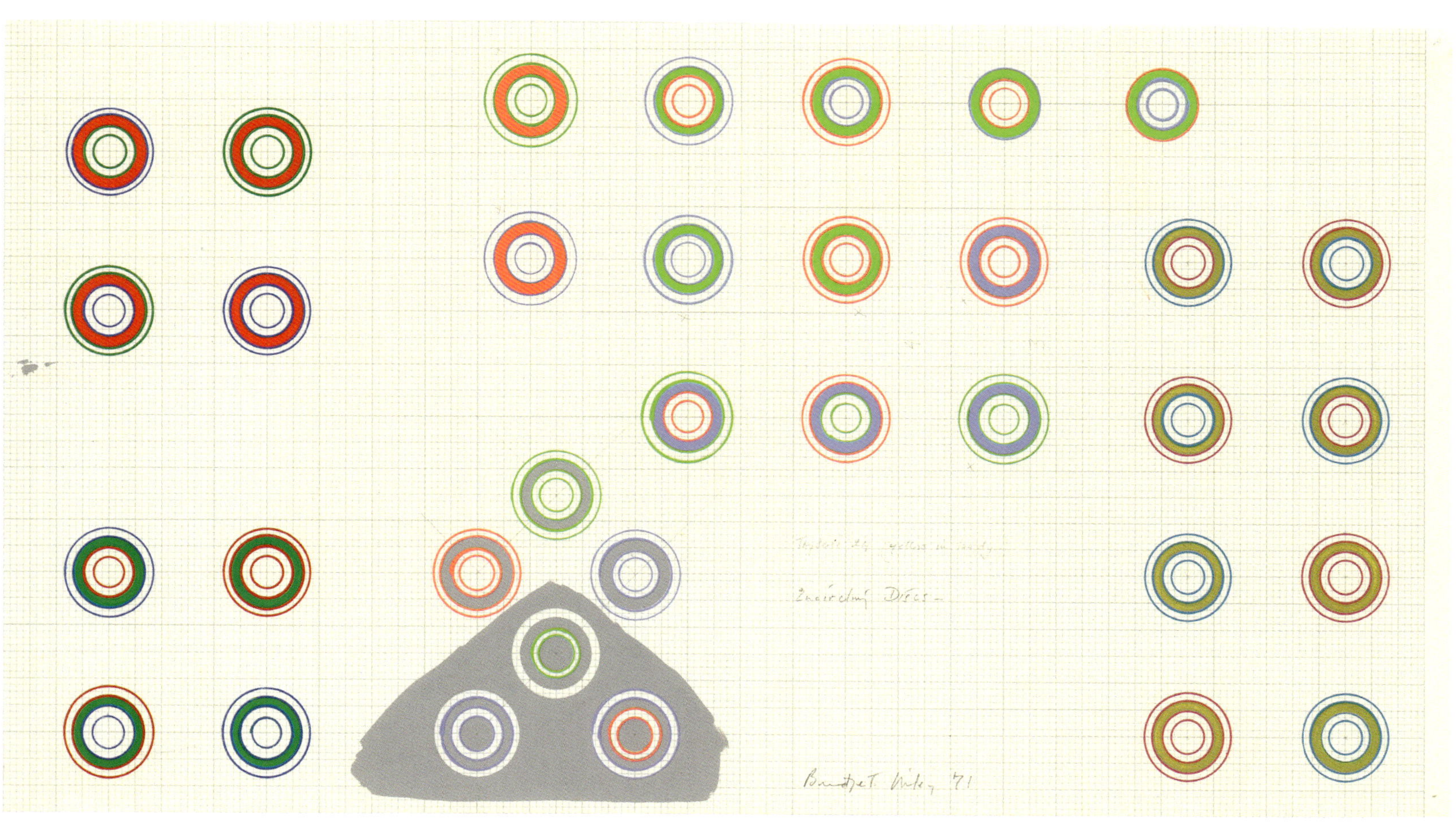

Encircling Discs With Grey in Grey to Black Sequence 1970
Gouache on paper
16¾ × 35¼ inches

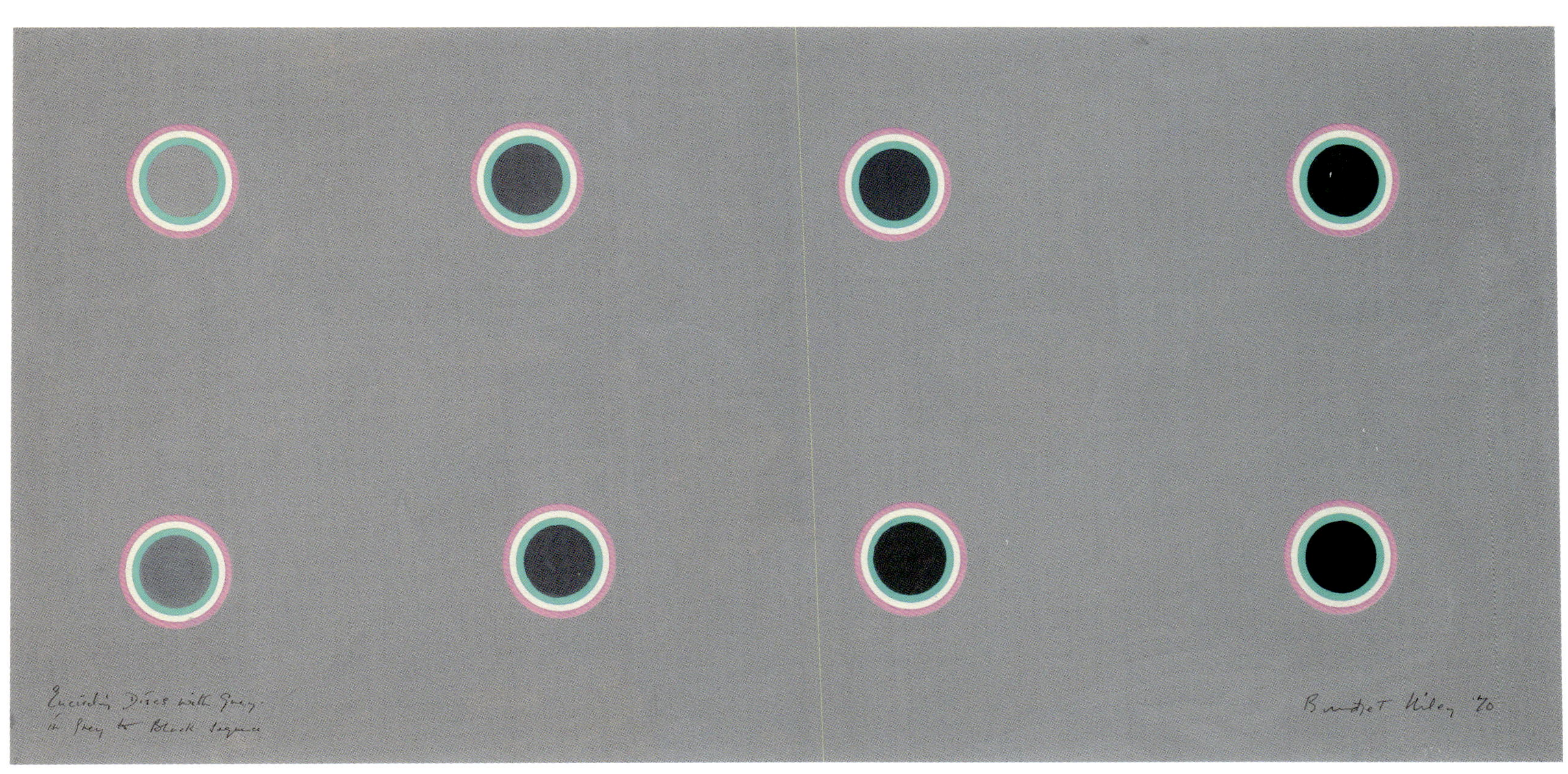

Euclidian Discs with Grey.
in Grey to Black sequence
Bridget Riley '70

Encircling Discs with Black 1970
Gouache on paper
9¾ × 14¼ inches

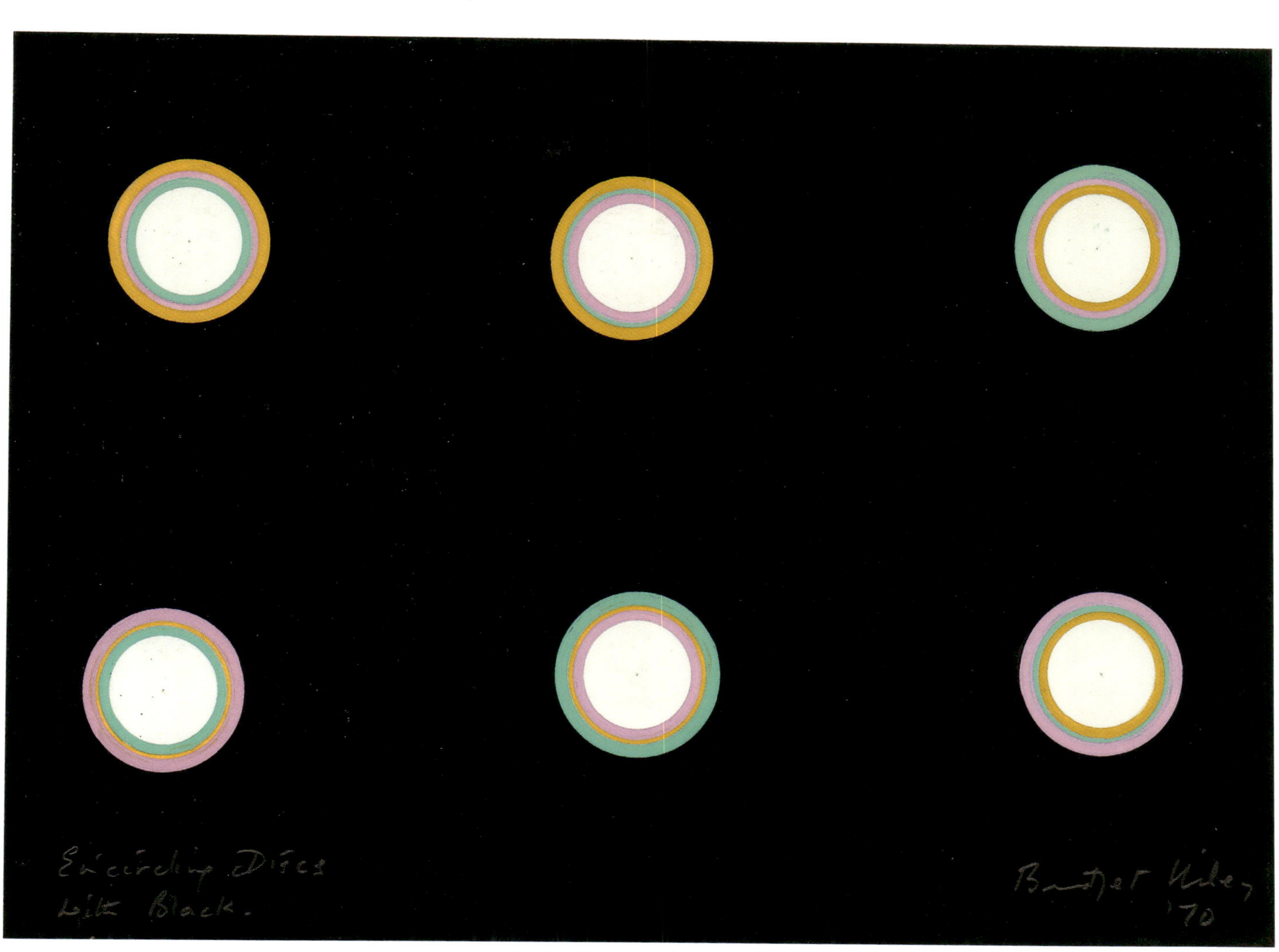

Encircling Discs
with Black.
Bridget Riley
'70

Coloured Greys 1971
Gouache and pencil on paper
27¼ × 18 inches

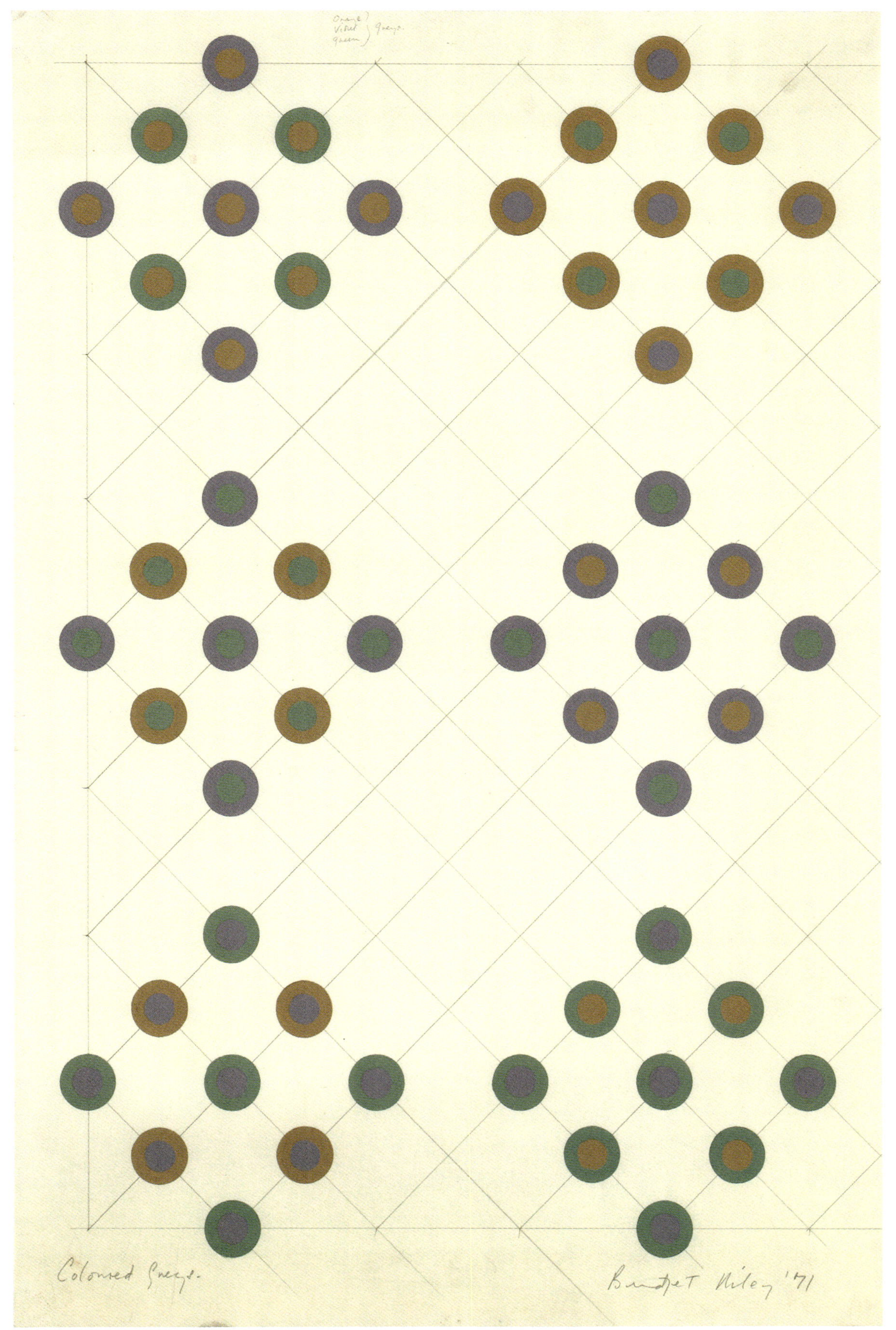
Orange)
Viridi) Greys.
green)
Coloured Greys.
Bridget Riley '71

Untitled 1970
Gouache on paper
24 × 26½ inches

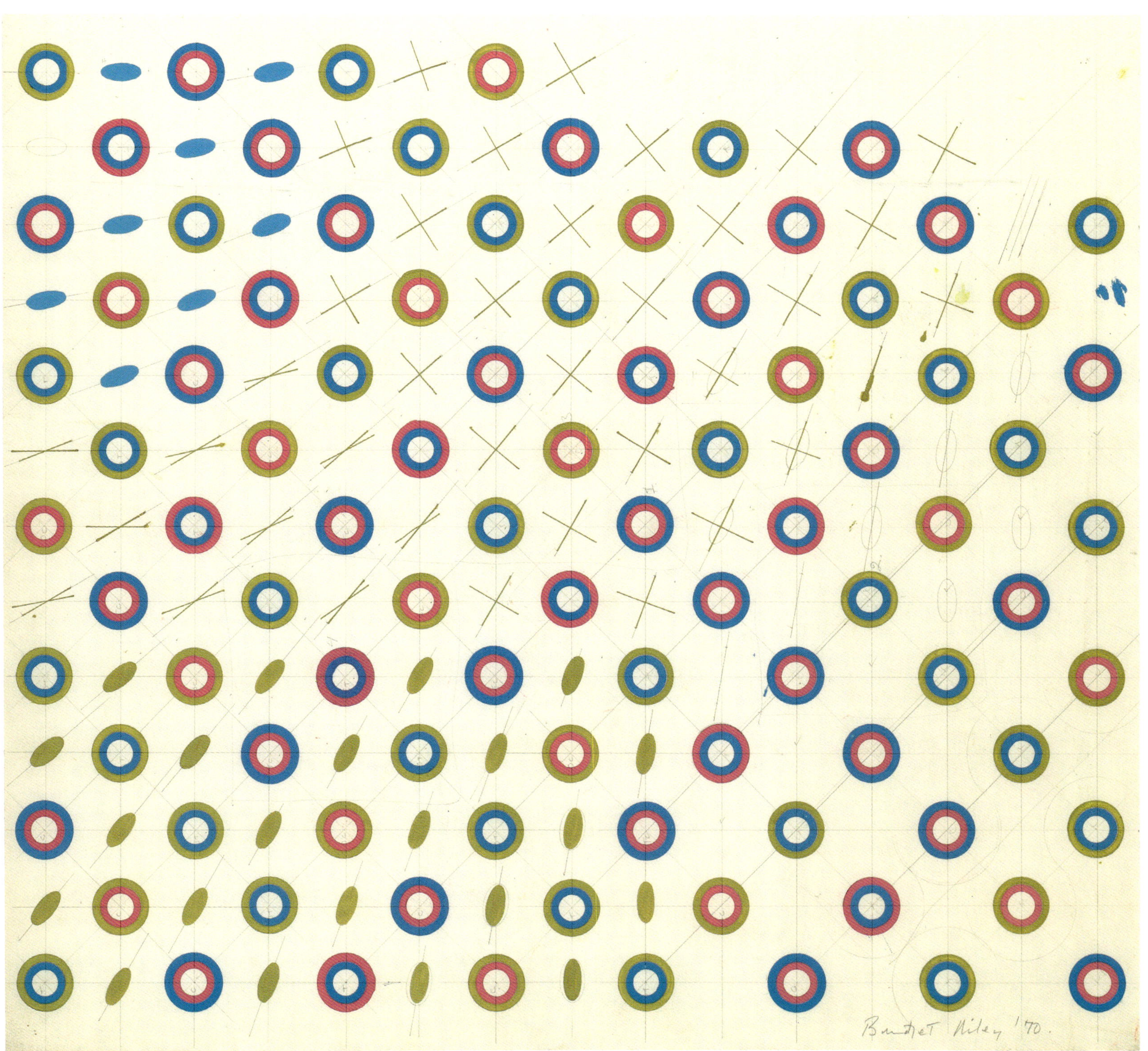

Bridget Riley '70.

Closed Discs: Turquoise, Cerise, Ochre 1970
Gouache and pencil on paper
26 × 21 inches

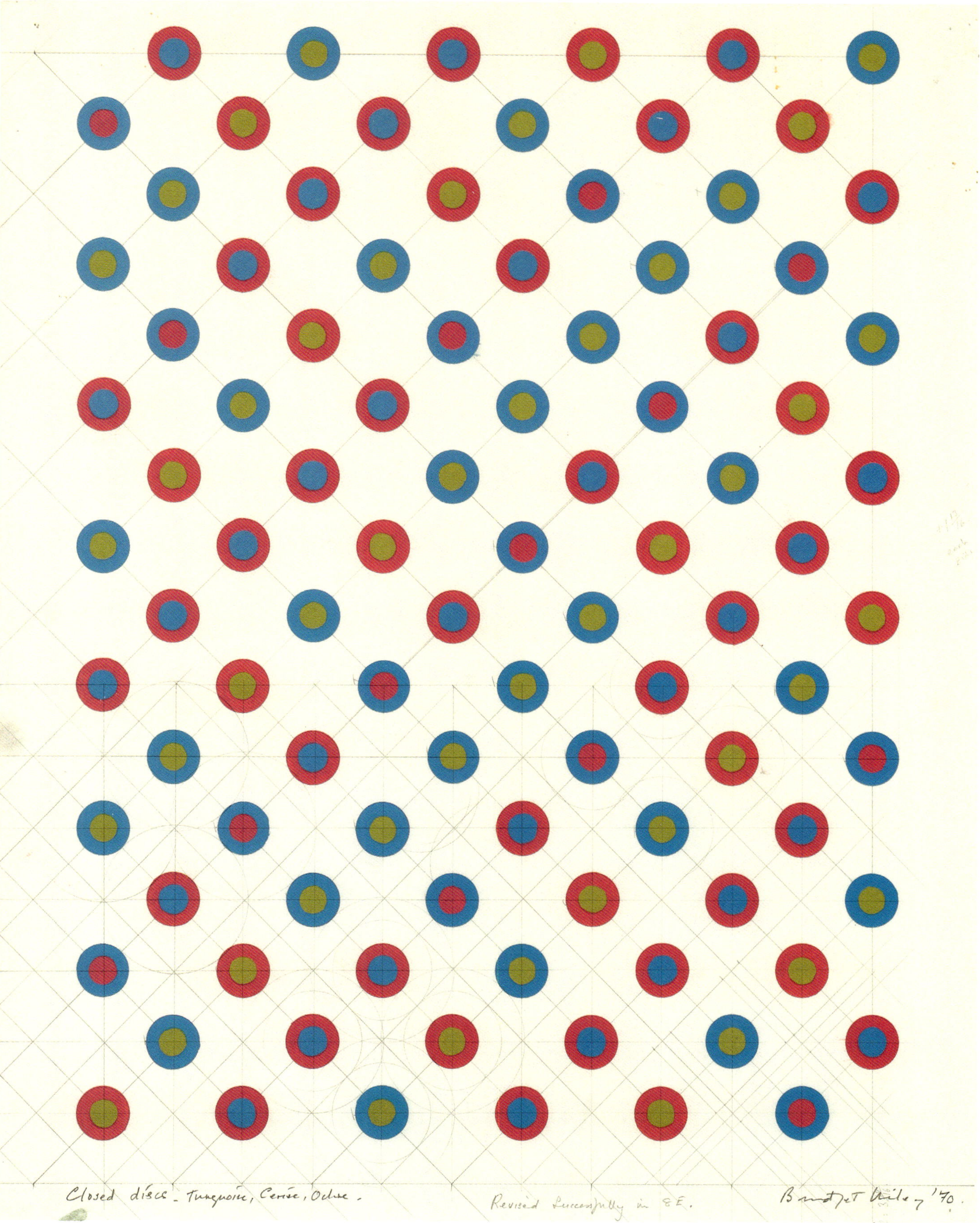

Closed discs - Turquoise, Cerise, Ochre.
Revised successfully in BE.
Bridget Riley '70.

Light Red, Blue, Green: Dispersal Study 1970
Gouache and pencil on paper
29¾ × 22¾ inches

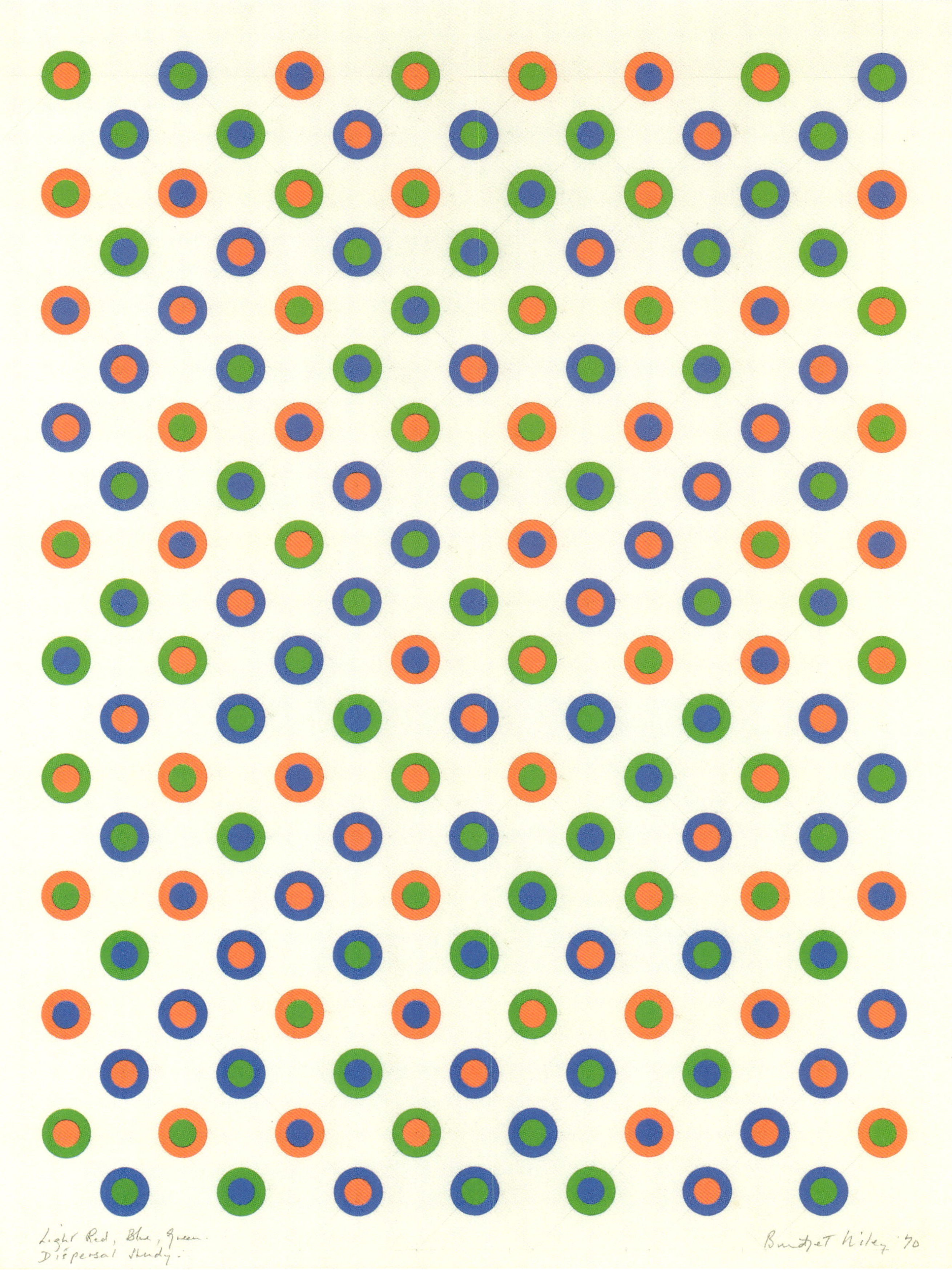
Light Red, Blue, Green.
Dispersal Study.
Bridget Riley '70

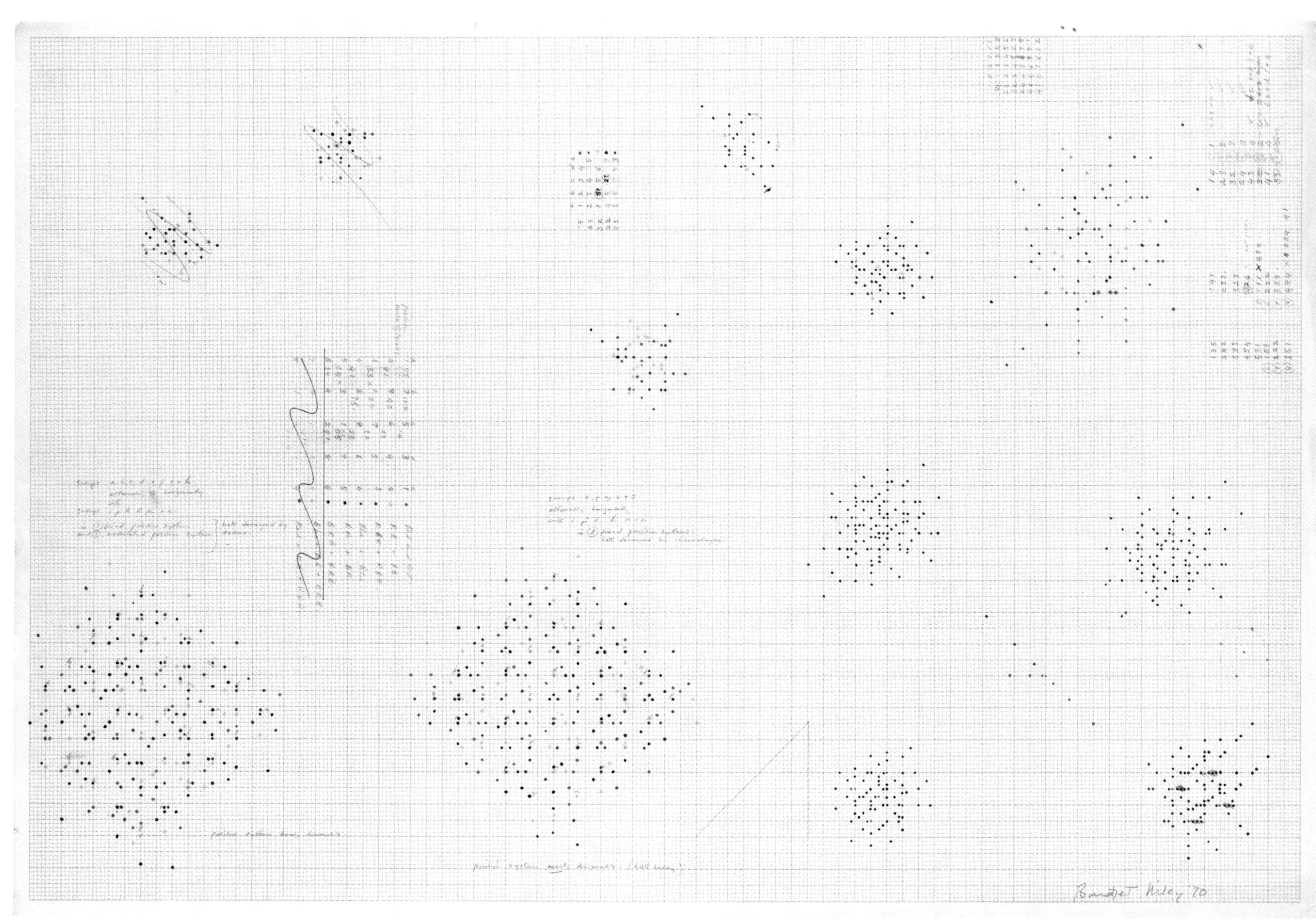

Untitled 1970
Pencil and felt-tip pen on graph paper
28 × 41 inches

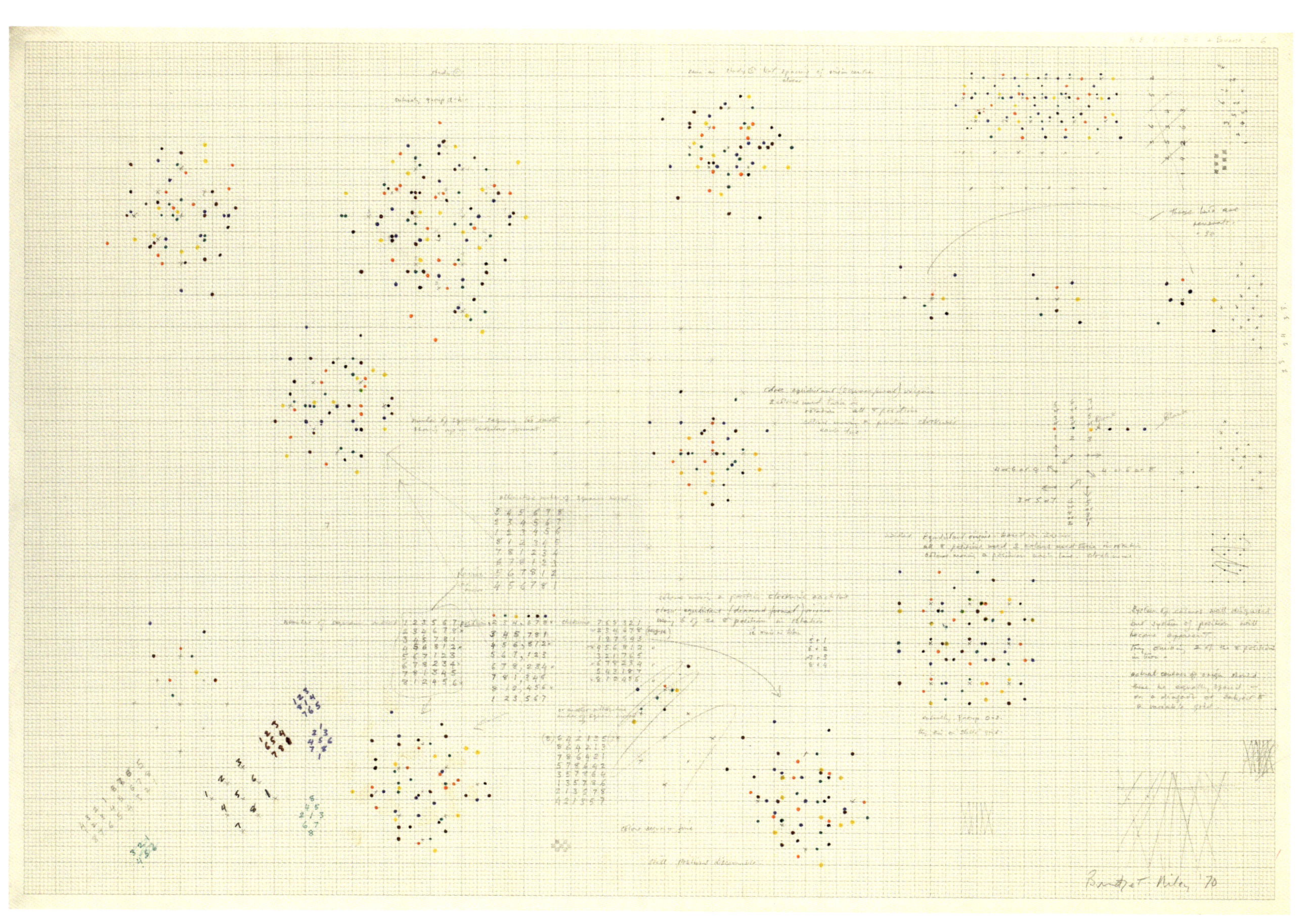

Untitled 1970
Pencil and felt-tip pen on graph paper
28 × 41 inches

Published on the occasion of

**Bridget Riley
Circles Colour Structure
Studies 1970/71**

at Karsten Schubert
19 November 2008 – 30 January 2009

Published in 2008 by
Ridinghouse / Karsten Schubert
5–8 Lower John Street
Golden Square
London W1F 9DR
www.karstenschubert.com

Distributed in the UK and Europe by
Cornerhouse
70 Oxford Street
Manchester M15 5NH
www.cornerhouse.org

Distributed in the US by
RAM Publications
2525 Michigan Avenue Building A2
Santa Monica CA 90404
www.rampub.com

Interview © 2008 Robert Kudielka and Bridget Riley
'In Conversation with Robert Kudielka' was first published in German
translation in the exhibition catalogue *Bridget Riley*, Kunstverein Göttingen,
1972, pp. 4–10. The English original appeared a year later in *Bridget Riley:
Paintings and Drawings, 1961–1973*, exhibition catalogue, Arts Council of Great
Britain, 1973, pp. 9–13. It was then reprinted in *The Eye's Mind: Bridget Riley
Collected Writings 1965–1999*, edited by Robert Kudielka, 1999, Thames &
Hudson, pp. 80–86.

Images © 2008 Bridget Riley

British Library Cataloguing-in-Publication Data
A full catalogue record of this book is available from the British Library

ISBN 978-1-905464-19-7

Ridinghouse Editor: Rosalind Horne

Design: Tim Harvey

Print: Balding + Mansell, Norwich

Front endpaper
Untitled 1970 (detail)
Pencil and felt-tip pen on graph paper

Back endpaper
Untitled 1970 (detail)
Pencil and felt-tip pen on graph paper

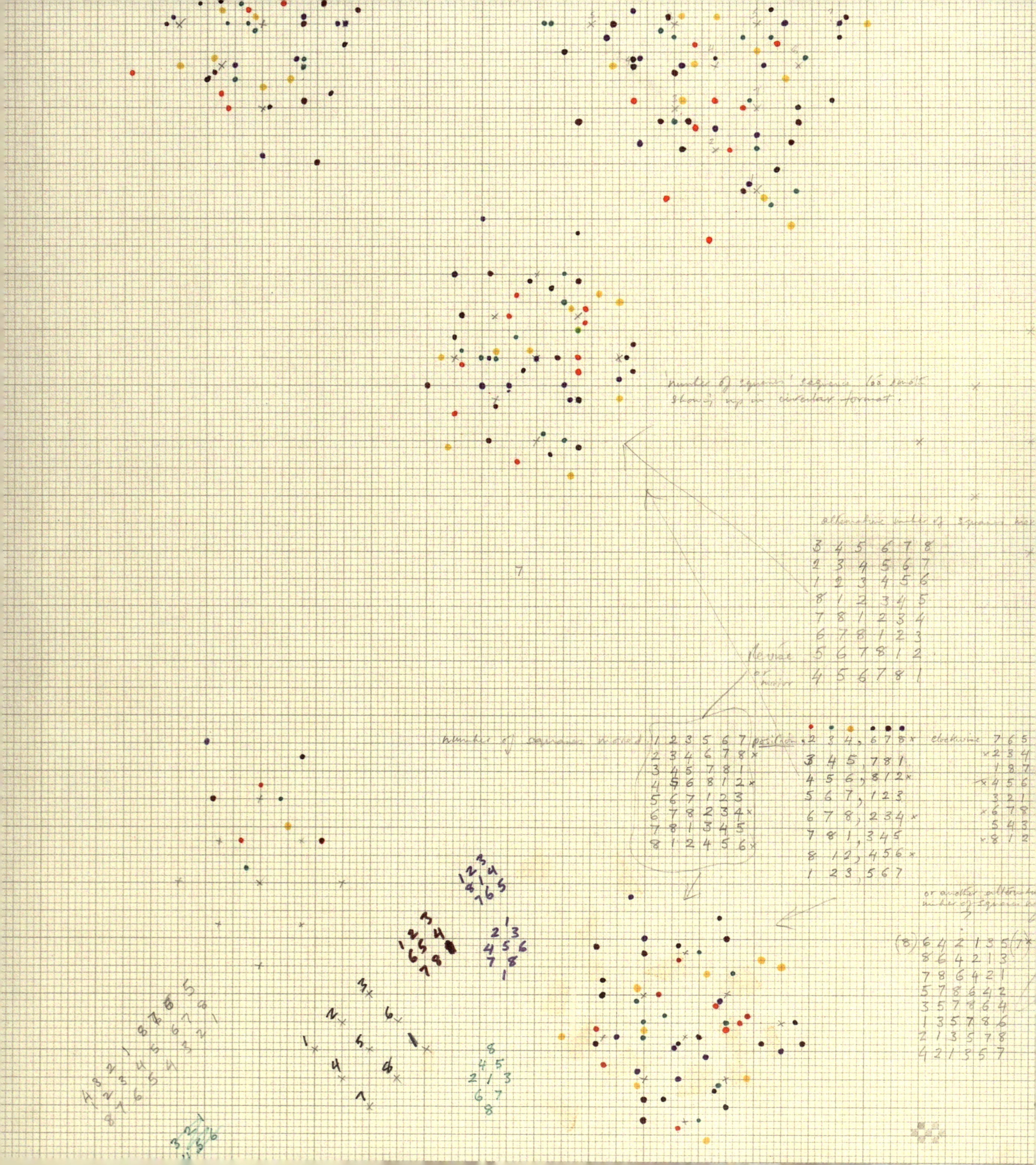

'number of squares' sequence too small showing up in circular format.

alternative number of squares ke...
3 4 5 6 7 8
2 3 4 5 6 7
1 2 3 4 5 6
8 1 2 3 4 5
7 8 1 2 3 4
6 7 8 1 2 3
5 6 7 8 1 2
4 5 6 7 8 1
Revise or major

number of squares rotated
1 2 3 5 6 7   position   2 3 4, 6 7 8 x   clockwise   7 6 5
2 3 4 6 7 8 x   3 4 5, 7 8 1   x 2 3 4
3 4 5 7 8 1   4 5 6, 8 1 2 x   1 8 7
4 5 6 8 1 2 x   5 6 7, 1 2 3   x 4 5 6
5 6 7 1 2 3   6 7 8, 2 3 4 x   3 2 1
6 7 8 2 3 4 x   7 8 1, 3 4 5   x 6 7 8
7 8 1 3 4 5   8 1 2, 4 5 6 x   5 4 3
8 1 2 4 5 6 x   1 2 3, 5 6 7   x 8 1 2

or another alternative number of squares ?
(8) 6 4 2 1 3 5 (7) x
8 6 4 2 1 3
7 8 6 4 2 1
5 7 8 6 4 2
3 5 7 8 6 4
1 3 5 7 8 6
2 1 3 5 7 8
4 2 1 3 5 7